DRAWING LEGENDARY MONSTERS
DRAWING WEREWOLVES
AND OTHER GOTHIC GHOULS

Steve Beaumont

PowerKiDS press™

New York

Published in 2011 by The Rosen Publishing Group, Inc.
29 East 21st Street, New York, NY 10010

Artwork and text: Steve Beaumont and Dynamo Limited
Editors: Kate Overy and Joe Harris
U.S. editor: Kara Murray
Designer: Steve Flight

Library of Congress Cataloging-in-Publication Data

Beaumont, Steve.
 Drawing werewolves and other gothic ghouls / by Steve Beaumont.
     p. cm. — (Drawing legendary monsters)
 Includes index.
   ISBN 978-1-4488-3254-5 (library binding) — ISBN 978-1-4488-3255-2 (pbk.) — ISBN 978-1-4488-3256-9 (6-pack)
 1. Werewolves in art—Juvenile literature. 2. Horror in art—Juvenile literature. 3. Drawing—Technique—Juvenile literature. I. Title.
 NC825.M6B44 2011
 743'.87—dc22

                                    2010025758

Printed in China
SL001631US

CPSIA Compliance Information: Batch #WA11PK: For Further Information contact Rosen Publishing, New York, New York at 1-800-237-9932

CONTENTS

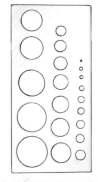

GETTING STARTED

Before you can start creating fantastic artwork, you need some basic supplies. Take a look at this guide to help you get started.

PAPER

Layout Paper

It's a good idea to buy inexpensive plain paper from a stationery shop for all of your practice work. Most professional illustrators use cheaper paper for basic layouts and practice sketches, before producing their final artworks on more costly paper.

Heavy Drawing Paper

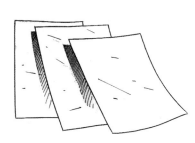

Heavy-duty, high-quality drawing paper is ideal for your final drawings. You don't have to buy the most expensive brand – most art or craft shops will stock their own brand or a student brand. Unless you're thinking of turning professional, these will do just fine.

Watercolor Paper

This paper is made from 100 percent cotton, so it is much higher quality than wood-based paper. Most art shops stock a large range of weights and sizes. Using 140-pound (300 gsm) paper will be fine.

PENCILS

Buy a variety of graphite (lead) pencils ranging from soft (#1) to hard (#4). Hard pencils last longer and leave less lead on the paper. Soft pencils leave more lead and wear down quickly. #2 pencils are a good medium option to start with. Spend time drawing with each pencil and get used to its qualities.

Another product to try is the mechanical pencil, in which you click the lead down the barrel using the button at the top. Try 0.5mm lead thickness to start with. These pencils are good for fine detail work.

CIRCLE TEMPLATE

This is useful for drawing small circles.

FRENCH CURVES

These are available in several shapes and sizes and are useful for drawing curves.

INKING AND COLORING

Once you have finished your pencil drawing, you need to add ink and color. Here are some tools you can use to get different results.

PENS
There are plenty of high-quality pens on the market these days that will do a decent job of inking. It's important to experiment with a range of different ones to decide with which ones you are comfortable working.

You may find you end up using a combination of pens to produce your finished artworks. Remember to use a pen with waterproof ink if you want to color your illustrations with a watercolor or ink wash. It's usually a good idea to use waterproof ink anyway as there's nothing worse than having your nicely inked drawing ruined by an accidental drop of water!

PANTONE MARKERS
These are versatile, double-ended pens that give solid, bright colors. You can use them as you would regular marker pens or with a brush and a little water like a watercolor pen.

BRUSHES
Some artists like to use a fine brush for inking linework. This takes a bit more practice and patience to master, but the results can be very satisfying. If you want to try your hand at brushwork, you should invest in some high-quality sable brushes.

WATERCOLORS AND GOUACHE
Most art stores stock a wide range of these products, from professional to student quality.

MASTER CLASS: EVIL HANDS

Here we will look at how you can turn a drawing of a human hand into that of a monster, by simply thickening or thinning the shape.

The pictures below show the basic construction of a human hand.

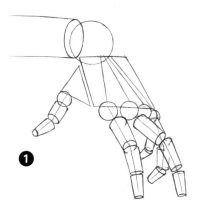

1

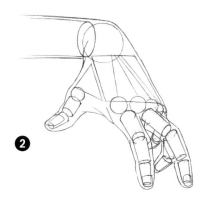

2

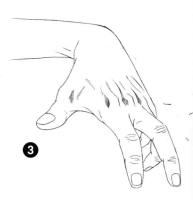

3

Picture 1 By thickening the palm and the digits and adding hair and claws, you can turn the human hand into that of a werewolf (see below).

Picture 2 By thinning the overall shape and adding long, narrow nails, the hand begins to take on the appearance of a vampire's (below).

Picture 3 You can exaggerate the shape of the hand, fingers, and nails to create a more nightmarish version (below).

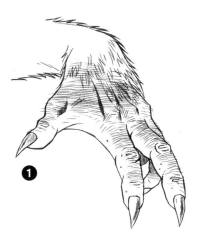

1

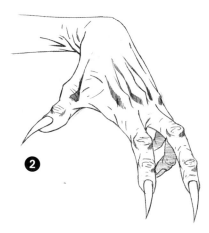

2

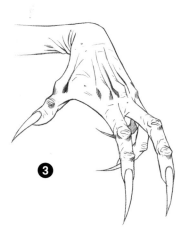

3

MASTER CLASS: BEASTLY HEADS

Let's take a closer look at drawing the head of the zombie found on pages 20–25.

Picture 1 Start with the basic oval shape for the head and map out the grid for the eyes, nose, and mouth.

Picture 2 Draw in the features. The eyes are sunken, the nose has caved in, and the skin is stretched tight across the skull.

Picture 3 Define the jawline and add the teeth and unkempt hair.

Picture 4 Now add shading and detail to the skin. Notice the dark shading around the eyes to create that sunken look and the tightness of the skin around the cheekbones and mouth.

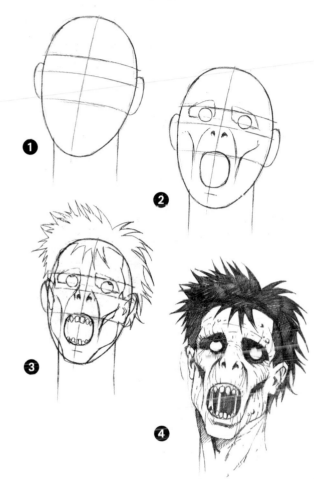

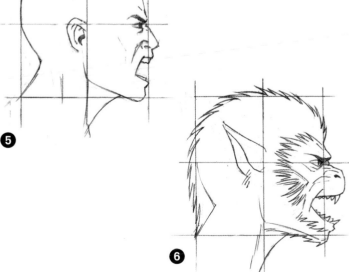

Picture 5 shows a profile of a human head. In Picture 6 the human head has been distorted and turned into a beast. Notice how the brow and the areas around the nose and mouth have been extended for an animalistic effect.

VAMPIRE

Eastern Europe's most infamous folkloric beast, the vampire, has a name as old as its myth. The word comes from *vampir*, the Hungarian word for "witch." These undead creatures feed on the blood of the living and can supposedly change from humans into bats. They sleep in coffins.

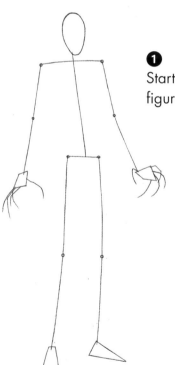

1

Start with the tall stick figure.

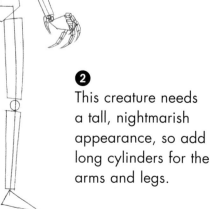

2

This creature needs a tall, nightmarish appearance, so add long cylinders for the arms and legs.

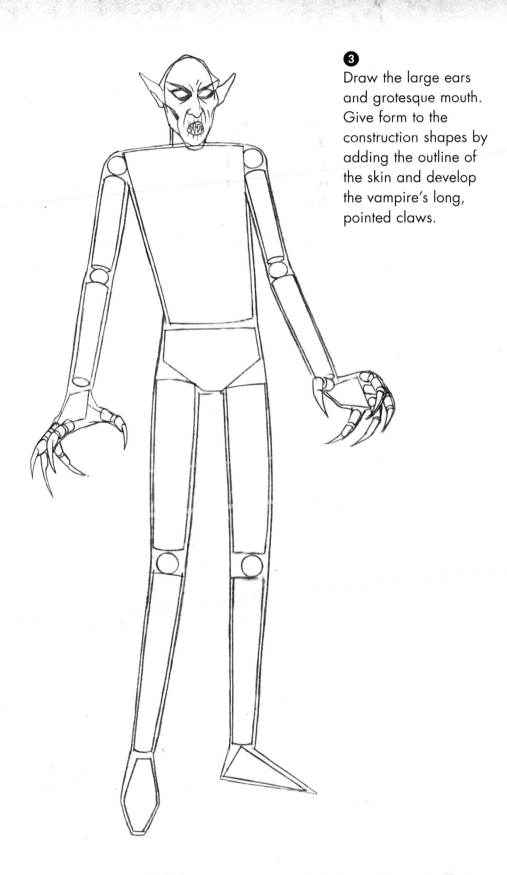

3 Draw the large ears and grotesque mouth. Give form to the construction shapes by adding the outline of the skin and develop the vampire's long, pointed claws.

TOP TIP
To make the coat look authentic, give it heavily padded shoulders and a big collar.

4
Add the outline of the vampire's trench coat and remove the construction shapes.

5
Finish the pencil drawing by adding more detail. Apply solid shading to the majority of the figure, leaving highlights around the edges und on the face.

6

Ink over the pencil drawing using large areas of flat, black color. Keep the spots on the hands and face.

VAMPIRE

Create darker areas around the eyes and finish off the face by making the eyes blood red.

7 When coloring the vampire, avoid using warm skin tones. Stick to pale grays and yellowish greens to create a ghoulish look.

Color the coat using a midrange gray base followed by layers of dark blue.

WEREWOLF

The werewolf was for centuries believed to prowl lands from Brazil to Russia. Like the vampire, it is the victim of a curse. Anyone who is bitten by this monster also becomes a werewolf, and on a full moon, they will turn into a half-human beast thirsty for blood.

1
Draw the stick figure in a threatening pose.

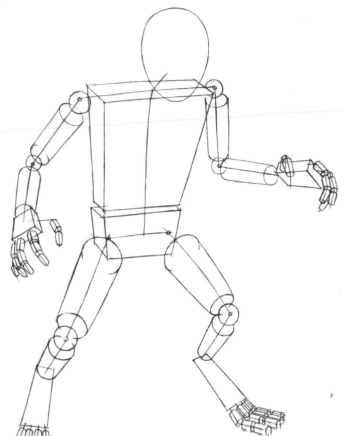

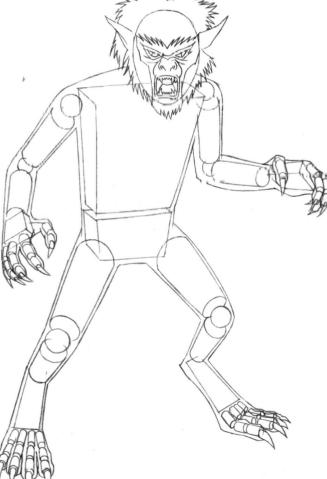

2
Construct the upper body using solid boxes. Use cylinders for the arms and legs, drawing larger ones for the upper legs, which are broad.

3
Draw the face and the outline of the skin around the construction shapes. Note that the head is like that of a human but with animal features.

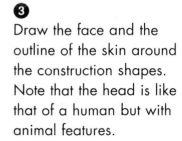

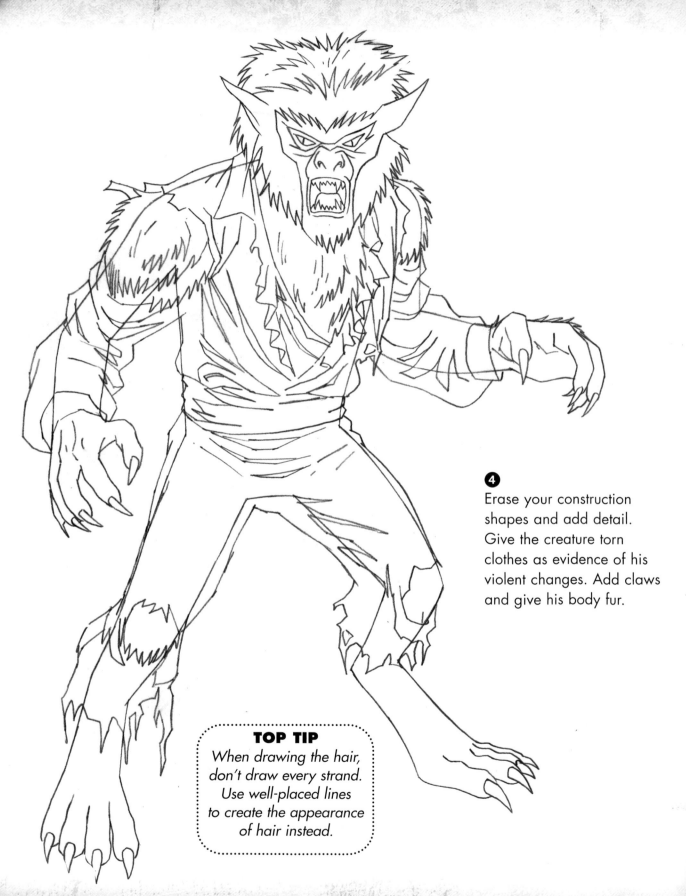

❹
Erase your construction shapes and add detail. Give the creature torn clothes as evidence of his violent changes. Add claws and give his body fur.

TOP TIP
When drawing the hair, don't draw every strand. Use well-placed lines to create the appearance of hair instead.

5 Add fine details and shading to create the final pencil drawing. Solid areas of shading in the hair creates volume and shape.

6
Ink over the pencil drawing. Use solid areas of black on the undersides of his arms, legs, and on his head.

7

It's time to color your werewolf, which will really bring him to life.

Color the fur using a midrange brown base and build up with darker layers of reddish brown. Blend in the darker areas using dark grays.

Color the shirt using very pale grays as a base, followed by layers of darker grays to create shaded areas. Use an olive green to color the torn pants. The claws are colored using a blend of grays and navy blue.

ZOMBIE

While the vampire is brilliantly smart and the werewolf has an animal intelligence, the zombie is a lumbering, mindless creature driven by only one emotion: its uncontrollable hunger. These grotesque, rotting creatures feel no pain, and they will continue their slow, relentless advance even if they lose limbs.

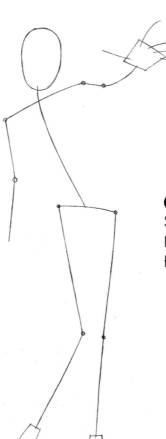

1

Start with the stick figure. Note that the left arm is foreshortened.

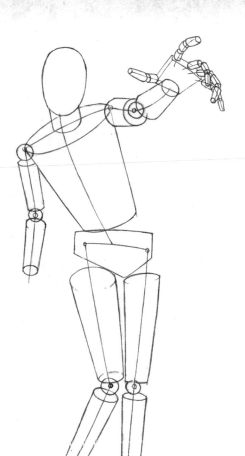

②
Now draw the cylindrical construction shapes. Short, fat cylinders are used on the left arm.

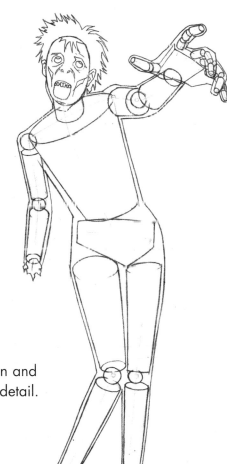

③
Add a layer of skin and the hair and face detail.

TOP TIP
The zombie has the face of someone who is undead. The eyes are sunken and dark, and all fluid has come out of the skin so it appears wrinkled. The teeth can be rotten, too.

Find out how to add gruesome detail to the zombie's face on page 7.

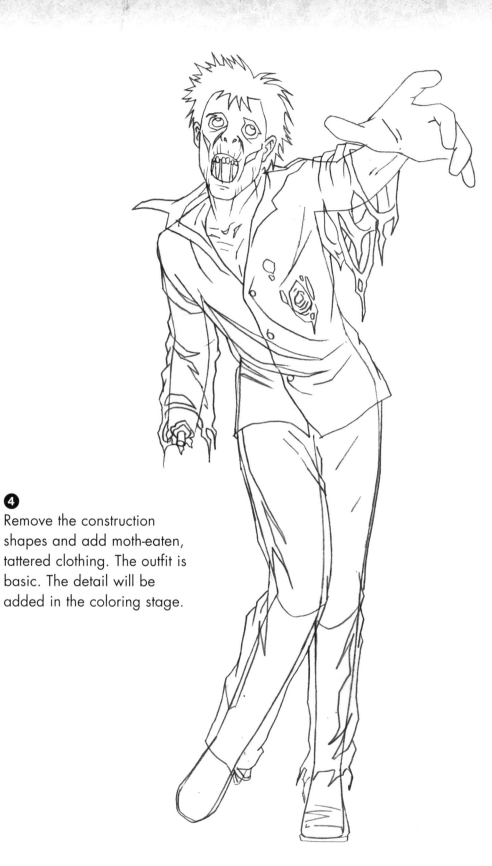

4

Remove the construction shapes and add moth-eaten, tattered clothing. The outfit is basic. The detail will be added in the coloring stage.

5

Add wrinkles to the face and darken the area around the eyes. Add shading around the cheeks to make them look sunken. Finish with some blocks of shading that will be solidly inked over.

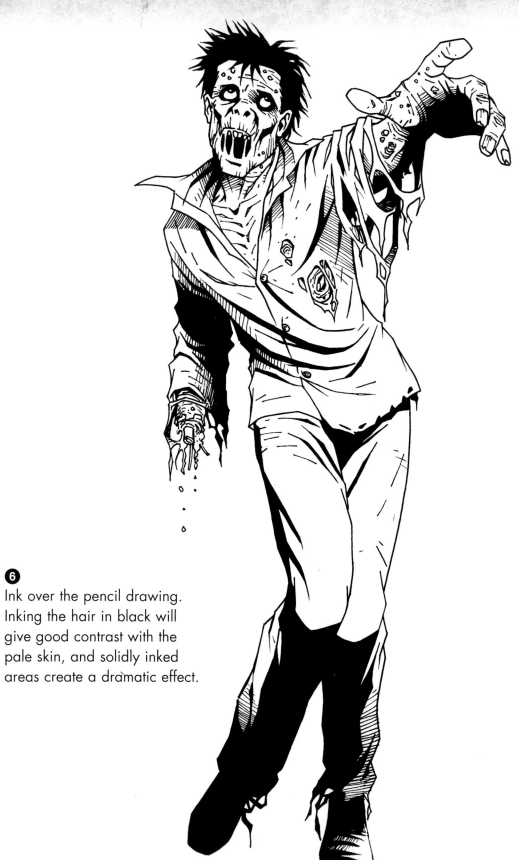

6

Ink over the pencil drawing. Inking the hair in black will give good contrast with the pale skin, and solidly inked areas create a dramatic effect.

7

Color the zombie, adding some gruesome color effects.

The skin should look lifeless, so stick to very pale (almost white) skin tones. Build up with layers of very pale gray and light greens.

Color the shirt in white, then add red blood stains. Color his pants using layers of dark gray.

TOP TIP
To create an aged, washed-out look, use a wet blender marker and daub the ink over the dried colors.

CREATING A SCENE: THE GOTHIC VILLAGE

A moonlit medieval village is the perfect scene for a tale of gothic horror. Just imagine: the townspeople are suddenly woken from their sleep by a bloodcurdling scream. Will they be able to drive away the creatures of the night with flaming torches and protective charms? Or will they fall victim, one by one, to the monsters hidden in the shadows?

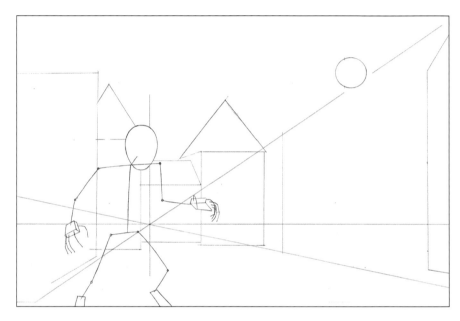

1 Sketch out some lines of perspective, coming together in a vanishing point. Remember to take into account where the werewolf will appear. Draw in some simple angular shapes that will make up the main buildings.

2 Create some variation in the skyline by using different-shaped roofs to represent cottages, barn-type buildings, and churches. Flesh out the background by adding some treetops, which will break up the straight lines of the roofs.

3 Add in the detail of your buildings. You can create a Gothic feel by drawing wooden frames on the outside of your buildings. Leafy treetops will add visual interest, giving your image a variety of different shapes and textures.

4 Fill in the ground area with beaten carriage tracks, patches of earth, and puddles of water to give it an authentic village feel. Don't forget that a werewolf needs a good moon to howl at. Nothing says Gothic like the silhouettes of bats in midair.

5 When inking your scene, remember that the full moon is your light source. That will help you figure out exactly where your shadows should be. Don't overdo the shadows. You can create the sense that it's nighttime by your choice of colors in the next stage.

6 Blue and purple are the colors to use when it comes to creating a spooky nighttime look. This can be contrasted with pools of yellow light streaming from the windows. When coloring around the moon and clouds, a gentle touch is required.

GLOSSARY

animalistic (a-nuh-muh-LIS-tik) Like an animal.

coffin (KAH-fun) A box that holds a dead body.

cylinder (SIH-lin-der) A shape with circular ends and straight lines.

develop (dih-VEH-lup) To further or continue something.

digit (DIJ-it) A finger or toe.

evidence (EH-vuh-dunts) Facts that prove something.

folkloric (FOHK-lawr) Belonging to folklore, the traditional stories and beliefs of a group of people.

lumber (LUM-ber) Move in an awkward way.

perspective (per-SPEK-tiv) Changing the size and shape of objects in an artwork to create a sense of nearness or distance.

unkempt (un-KEMPT) Scruffy and untidy.

vanishing point (VAN-ish-ing POYNT) The point at which the lines showing perspective in a drawing meet each other.

INDEX

WEB SITES

Due to the changing nature of internet links, PowerKids Press has developed an online list of Web sites related to the subject of this book. This site is updated regularly. Please use this link to access the list:
www.powerkidslinks.com/dlm/werewo/